A Sense OF PLACE
CONTEMPORARY NEEDLEWORK

*For Sarah,
with many thanks —
Oct 98
Alena.*

To my mother, Dahlia Pearl Douglas

A Sense OF PLACE
CONTEMPORARY NEEDLEWORK

COMPILED BY
Jerry Rogers

Angus&Robertson
An imprint of HarperCollins*Publishers*

AN ANGUS & ROBERTSON BOOK
An imprint of HarperCollinsPublishers

First published in Australia in 1992 by
CollinsAngus&Robertson Publishers Pty Limited (ACN 009 913 517)
A division of HarperCollinsPublishers (Australia) Pty Limited
25-31 Ryde Road, Pymble NSW 2073, Australia

HarperCollins Publishers (New Zealand) Limited
31 View Road, Glenfield, Auckland 10, New Zealand

HarperCollinsPublishers Limited
77-85 Fulham Palace Road, London W6 8JB, United Kingdom

Distributed in the United States of America by
HarperCollins Publishers
10 East 53rd Street, New York NY 10022, USA

Copyright © Jerry Rogers 1992

This book is copyright.
Apart from any fair dealing for the purposes of private study,
research, criticism or review, as permitted under the Copyright
Act, no part may be reproduced by any process without written
permission. Inquiries should be addressed to the publishers.

National Library of Australia
Cataloguing-in-Publication data:

Rogers, Jerry
    A sense of place: contemporary needlework.
    Bibliography.
    ISBN 0 207 16978 0
    1. Needlework - Australia - Pictorial works. II. Title.
746.40222

Typeset in Garamond 3 by High Q Resolutions Pty Ltd, Australia
Printed in the People's Republic of China.

5 4 3 2 1
96 95 94 93 92

Acknowledgments

I would like to thank Kim Anderson, the non-fiction publisher at Collins Angus & Robertson, for the opportunity to pay tribute to contemporary needleworkers in Australia and for her support and encouragement throughout the project. I would also like to thank Kate Evans, Sandra Rigby and Karen Carter for their valued consultations and their expertise in assembling the given material.

My thanks also to all artists in needlework who submitted their work for consideration in *A Sense of Place*. Without their cooperation this book would not have been possible.

Contents

Acknowledgments v

Introduction ix

Bibliography xiv

Katrina Collins
The rhythm of stitching
1

Emma Robertson
Seeds fallen from the stars
5

Mac Neil
The elegance of parrots
9

Jane Bailey
Embroidering the Pilbara
11

Cheryl Bridgart
Memories and changes
15

Moreen Clark
The call of the Flinders
17

Kristen Dibbs
Fascination with the tactile world
19

Patrick Snelling
A robust and wilful embellisher of surfaces
23

Angela Rossen
Style, tradition and method: a meeting
29

Helen Baldwin
Vastness and detail: the land and petit point
31

Pat Langford
Our allotted spaces
33

Contents

Rose Halliday-Smith
The fibrous untidiness of nature
37

Alvena Hall
Mystery and regeneration
39

Catherine O'Leary
Patterns in nature
43

Michaela Psaila-Savona
Carnivals of culture
45

Hester Hopkins
Co-operative creativity
49

Gabriella Verstraeten
Movement and abstraction
53

Heather Johns
Magic, ritual, ceremony
55

Annemieke Mein
A statement of respect and love
59

Paul O'Connor
The cultural rubbish dump of the soul
61

Judith Pinnell
Imperial treasures
67

Dorothy Roth
Searching for the essence
69

Doreen Curran
Distance, depth and dimension
71

Celia Player
Creation through destruction
73

Cynthia Sparks
Depths of design: weaving the rainforest
77

Mirjam Koenig
Silk magic
79

Wendy Wright
Fleeting memories
83

Helen Lancaster
Underwater places
85

The Macedonian Project
Piece by piece: images of community
89

Joan Chapple
Gentleness and strength
91

Pamela Gaunt
The celebration of raw edges
93

Heather Joynes
Texture, techniques, landscape
95

Inga Hunter
From the forest floor
97

Sonja Armstrong
The stitching of angels
101

Stephanie Wood
Dreaming interiors
103

GABRIELLA VERSTRAETEN **LUCY'S TRICK**
1991, 610mm x 435mm

machine embroidered, quilting, hand decorated and beaded
on silk, organza and lurex
photographer: Gene Verstraeten

INTRODUCTION

Over the past ten years there has been an explosion of interest in all forms of embroidery, needlework and stitchery. From suburban classes held at the local needlework shop to postgraduate degrees in textiles at universities, cloth, thread and fibre are offering an irresistible creative challenge. This ranges from a pleasurable pastime for some, to a form of self questioning and personal confrontation for others. The spectrum swings from a decorative approach and personal and domestic enhancement, to a high art form accepted and exhibited on prestigious gallery walls.

The materials encompass all fibres, textiles and threads, as well as non-traditional materials such as shells, feathers, bark, leaves, bone, teeth, beads, mirror and tassels. The techniques are many and varied. As an art form, the primacy of painting is being challenged by the extraordinary creativity of contemporary needleworkers.

Although dozens of needlework exhibitions are held every year throughout Australia, the extent and variety currently being practised has been only partially documented. Traditionally this has been the fate of most women's work in both mainstream areas of art and the so-called alternative forms which this publication addresses. *A Sense Of Place* may in a small way help to redress the balance.

My interest in needlework stems from childhood. One of my earliest memories is of my mother embroidering a white voile summer dress for me to wear. Between rows of insertion lace, over the shoulders and around the hemlines, she sewed tiny fields of golden lazy daisies. A former drover's wife, with many sons and only one daughter, my mother's endeavours to express herself artistically through needlework within a narrow, domestic confine, mirrored many other women's lives.

Anonymous, beautifully-wrought needlework of women from past generations, often discovered at markets and fetes, always tugs at my heart. Their artistic aspirations touch me deeply and hopes, dreams and personalities can be sensed in every stitch. Invariably I wander home with yet another doily, napkin or tablecloth to be mused over.

The origins of needlework in Australia can be found in the United Kingdom where ecclesiastical embroidery, under the generic term, *Opus Anglicanum,* established a tradition of excellence between the tenth and sixteenth centuries. Technically superb and extraordinarily expressive, embroidery was practised by both men and women and was considered an art form equivalent to painting and sculpture. The classic example is the *Bayeux Tapestry,* circa 1086, which records historic events from the accession of Edward the Confessor to the defeat of Harold at Hastings. Embroidered wool on linen, the work has been attributed to Queen Mathilda, consort of William the Conqueror, but in essence it was a workshop production of many hands.

Until the Renaissance, embroidery was politically and artistically a leading English art form sharing with the other arts the task of affirming the power of the Crown, Church and nobility. The dividing of media into crafts and fine art only commenced during the fifteenth and sixteenth centuries. At the same time, embroidery began its demise as an art form as social and economic changes began to categorise it as a domestic and feminine pursuit. Where embroidery was practised commercially, women were employed at the lowest levels.

During the next three centuries embroidery became a signifier of sexual difference and as it contracted in the commercial sphere, it expanded in the domestic arena. Here the patriarchally-approved feminine virtues of diligence, obedience, modesty, chastity and nurturance were inculcated through its practise. From the eighteenth century onwards embroidery was increasingly viewed in terms of what it displayed of the needleworker's femininity.

With the establishment of a convict colony in Australia in 1788, both the technical skills and the ideology of needlework were implanted in colonial society. No distinctive national style emerged, although some Australian imagery was evident by the mid-nineteenth century in the form of indigenous flora and fauna. However, throughout the nineteenth and twentieth centuries needlework developed as a highly skilled craft, sewing forming part of the school curricula and arts and crafts societies fostering the skill being founded.

The first dramatic change in the attitudes

CELIA PLAYER **TURNING POINT**
1990, 200mm x 270mm

hand painted and printed silk and silk chiffon, polyester lining fabrics, collage, machine embroidery

INTRODUCTION

to and the practise of needlework occurred in the early 1970s with artists taking an experimental and creative approach to this traditional art form. A new respect for and confidence in the art of needlework led to a plethora of new work, exhibitions and rising levels of expertise.

Today, as artists become more explorative and technically proficient, boundaries are being pushed further and further into more esoteric forms of personal expression.

Creative needleworkers such as Narelle Jubelin are now accepted as artists in their own right. Narelle epitomises a new breed of needleworker: physical and mental skills, fine aesthetic judgment in colour, texture and composition, patience during long training and assertive individuality of design combine to subvert the traditional image of embroidery. Through a critical and analytical approach, artists are using a socially-defined feminine skill both to

GABRIELLA VERSTRAETEN
MAGIC CARPET NO 1
1990, 400mm x 300mm
silk and taffeta appliqué on a satin base with lurex and organza, hand and machine embroidery
photographer: Gene Verstraeten

reflect society and to explore their own inner space.

The search for embroidery representative of this vast contemporary scene has led me to contact craft councils and embroidery guilds in each State, textile departments at many colleges of advanced education, TAFEs and universities throughout Australia. I have attended many exhibitions, spoken to loosely-banded groups of creative needleworkers as well as perused the work of many individuals quietly working on their own. I've been especially pleased to discover a number of men practising canvas and machine embroidery, although the numbers practising traditional embroidery remain small.

I would like to thank all the contributing artists to this publication and the many other talented needleworkers who took the time and trouble to forward examples of their work. A much larger volume would be necessary to do justice to the range of work being attempted in this field today. *A Sense Of Place* is but a small beginning.

Jerry Rogers

BIBLIOGRAPHY

Fletcher, M.　　*Needlework in Australia*
　　　　　　　(Oxford UniversityPress, Australia, 1989).

Greer, G.　　　*The Obstacle Race*
　　　　　　　(Secker & Warburg, London, 1979).

Parker, R.　　　*The Subversive Stitch – Embroidery and the Making of the Feminine*
　　　　　　　(Women's Press, Great Britian, 1984).

UP TO MARGARET STREET
1991, 500mm x 800mm

hand and machine embroidery, silk and clay tiles

A SENSE OF PLACE

UP TO MARGARET STREET
1986, 1m x 1.5m

acrylic/mixed media

Katrina Collins

The rhythm of stitching

As a child I used to sit and listen to my grandmother tell stories. All the while she talked she put her needle in and out of the canvas, with the rhythm of her stitching matching the rhythm of her speech. She invented her own tapestries of flowers, fruit, still life and birds. As I sat I too began to stitch and invent wild embroideries, patchwork and appliqué using whatever scraps of wool and fabric I could find.

Thus, Katrina Collins explains her introduction to embroidery. The urge to stitch has remained with her. Living in Rozelle, Sydney, she finds a lot of inspiration from the colour and excitement of the inner city. Her work has always been about her immediate, often domestic, environment:

Subjects such as views through the window, intimate spaces in my home, portraits of family and friends, have been my obsession.

Later work became more abstract, combining different images into one piece. A range of needlework techniques appear, and a variety of media: drawing, painting and collage, petit point, stitching, appliqué and appliqué netting give a vividness, a sense of movement, to this intimate and urban world. Her grandmother still provides direction and inspiration:

Her stories resound in my head, her domestic life reflected in my own: the security and love of the familiar environment.

CONTEMPORARY NEEDLEWORK

◄ EASTER SHOW NO 1
1983, 220mm x 330mm

painting/mixed media

▲ FUNFARE NO 2: KEWPIE DOLL
(Detail) 1983, 200mm x 300mm

embroidery, polished cotton

Emma Robertson

Seeds fallen from the stars

The universe and space discoveries, particularly the journey of the Voyager spacecraft, hold a particular fascination for Emma Robertson. The three works pictured are all explorations of the theme.

The linear patterns and circular shapes of the Olympus Mons Crater on the planet Mars inspired the work of the same name. Silk and cotton fabric was bonded onto a pale backing fabric. It was then embroidered using a Schiffili machine that creates a repeating pattern or design. The process of bonding and embroidery was repeated using straight and satin stitch on a sewing machine.

In *Moon Surface* Emma wanted to capture the rich textural surface, lines caused by craters and the movement of dust across the moon's surface observed from photographs and maps of the moon. The work was made from bonded silk, cotton and velvet and was embroidered using a Cornelly machine for the corded lines and a domestic sewing machine.

'Learned men argued that fossils had grown in the Earth from seeds fallen from the stars.' This quote explaining the existence of fossils, together with her own observation of a meteor shower, inspired Emma to create *Seeds Fallen from the Stars*. It shows two shooting stars falling to earth to create a fossil of a fish and leaf. It is machine and hand embroidered onto paper made by Emma from plant fibres. Gouache and enamel paint are also used.

OLYMPUS MONS CRATER *(Detail)*
1986, 904mm x 700mm
silk and cotton, bonded and machine stitchery

A SENSE OF PLACE

▲ SEEDS FALLEN FROM THE STARS *(Detail)*
1991, 200mm x 400mm

machine and hand embroidery, gouache and enamel paint

▶ MOON SURFACE *(Detail)*
1986, 707mm x 606mm

bonded silk, cotton and velvet, machine stitching

Mac Neil

The elegance of parrots

The beauty of the King parrot prompted Mac Neil to undertake what is almost a scientific study of their habits and physical features in needlework. Living on the verge of a large Eucalypt forest, she had the opportunity to observe the parrots at close range:

To me, their brilliant plumage and elegant shape were the ideal subject for the main work in an exhibition. Watching a flock of them banqueting in the garden, the mature males, with their brilliant scarlet and green colours, stood out from the other family members as the most appealing. An upside down parrot fitted well with the design — parrots are often seen hanging from a branch in what appears to be a very playful attitude; in fact they are usually gathering seeds or blossoms for their dinner and hang there feeding, quite unperturbed.

The design was first worked out on paper and then transferred to calico and completed in embroidery with a single strand of stranded embroidery cotton.

KING PARROT AND JUNIOR
1991, 310mm x 220mm

stranded embroidery cotton on calico

JANE BAILEY

Embroidering the Pilbara

For the past three and a half years Jane Bailey has lived in Karratha, a small town in the remote north west region of Western Australia — the Pilbara.

The landscape and extreme isolation made a powerful impact: *Karratha is dry and has a desert-like landscape. It has a definite strength and unique beauty, yet it seems to ooze with feelings of eeriness and a message which tells me that I don't belong here.*

The Sentence depicts her reactions to this isolation, and to personal circumstances that gave her no way out.

Using hand embroidery brings me closer to the emotion intended, she says. *I feel that by embroidering by hand I am putting more of myself into the piece; the feelings are coming straight from my heart into my hands and onto the fabric.*

Thus while most of the work was machine embroidered using the free arm technique, with the stitching built up repeatedly, the large face in the bottom of the picture was embroidered by hand. The fabric was dyed in fibre reactive dyes, cut out and pieced, and then appliquéd onto black fabric.

Jane describes her choice of needlework as an art form as an unconscious one:
I have always loved fabrics, but the main reason for my choice is that being a woman, I feel a kinship, an affinity with these particular tools. Embroidery and fabrics seem, for me, to go hand in hand with women and feminity.

THE SENTENCE
2400mm x 1030mm

machine and hand embroidery, procion dyed cotton

A SENSE OF PLACE

▲
SORROW'S SHADOW *(Detail)*
1600mm x 1100mm

machine embroidery, indigo dyed cotton and silk,
metallic rayon thread

▶
MOODS *(Detail)*
560mm x 390mm

permaset paints, cotton, machine embroidery,
balsa wood frame

A SENSE OF PLACE

MEMORIES AND CHANGES
1988, 750mm x 610mm

free machine embroidery with appliqué
photographer: Carmel Bridgart

CHERYL BRIDGART

Memories and changes

Cheryl Bridgart took up free machine embroidery as an experimental alternative to painting. She became fascinated by the tactile quality of fabric and thread, rich colour and surface texture and is now committed to producing both embroidered garments and pieces designed for hanging.

She finds the human form, especially the face, a constant source of inspiration. Faces on garments are particularly entertaining and challenging, for *they force people to rethink their approach to wearable fashion, to take notice, to amuse, and even to attract.* Many hours are spent embroidering each piece, creating detail and depth, exploring 'reality':

I become completely absorbed in the detail, the play of colour that I can achieve with free machine embroidery and threads, especially as I don't use paint, printed bases or dyes on my work.

To create the facial detail in *Memories and Changes,* the sewing machine was continually rethreaded with subtle changes of colour to create realism. Twelve different flesh tones were used on the hand of the old man in the foreground to create wrinkles, sunspots and skin texture.

The unifying aim in all Cheryl's work is to break down some of barriers against the acceptance of needlework as art:

I want to expand beyond the boundaries of established art forms and bridge the gap between craft and art.

A SENSE OF PLACE

THERE'S A PLACE WHERE
FLOWERS GROW AND THE BIRDS
FLY WILD AND FREE *(Detail)*

1990, full length coat

wool embroidery on hand knitted wool

MOREEN CLARK

The call of the Flinders

Moreen Clark's embroidered coat took over four months to complete and there were times, as she sat in summer temperatures of 45 degrees celsius with a woollen coat on her lap, when she wondered why she'd ever begun it.

She chose to depict a typical spring scene from the Flinders Ranges in South Australia, wanting to capture the golden wattles in bloom, and the purple and blue wash of Salvation Jane (or Patterson's Curse) over the slopes.

The coat is knitted in rough, handspun wool, chosen because of its rich texture and because it made a strong background for the heavy embroidery. Fleeces were chosen from a friend's farm, soon after the shearing:

The wool comes from several fleeces — white, oatmeal, soft greys and browns. I chose fleeces that are both soft and lustrous because I like the sheen for the flowers and leaves. Greys overdyed give soft muted greens and blues and lovely distant mountain colours.

During the dyeing process, colour variations were planned, and the wool dipped as many as four times to get the right tone. This speeded up the needlework as the thread colour did not need to be changed quite so often. It also gave the light and shade in grasses and bushes.

Moreen doesn't use patterns or graphs when she begins to knit — it is done freestyle. The embroidery stitches are simple, locking into the knitting to form part of the overall fabric. Beads — silvery and sugary — accent centres of the flowers and sparkle as they catch the light.

I've called my coat 'There's a place where the flowers grow and the birds fly wild and free'. That's the call of the Flinders.

A SENSE OF PLACE

ROCKY CREEK *(Detail)*
1987, 300mm x 200mm

*machine embroidery and appliqué, naphthol dyed
silk, silk organza, plastic, aluminium foil,
string, synthetic quilt batting, polyester
machine threads
photographer: Richard Dibbs*

KRISTEN DIBBS

Fascination with the tactile world

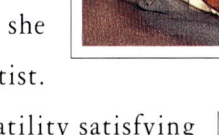

Trained as an artist and teacher, Kristen Dibbs has always been fascinated with the tactile world, but it wasn't until she began experimenting with a sewing machine that she became a dedicated textile artist. She finds its speed and versatility satisfying and rewarding.

Kristen prefers to work intuitively, inspired by the textures of the natural world — rocks, moss, anything with a rich and intricate surface: *I rarely sketch an idea first — usually I collect fabrics in related colours and begin playing with them until an idea begins to form.*

Rocky Creek began as an abstract arrangement of colour and texture, inspired by rock strata in sandstone, and only developed into a specific subject as work continued.

Recycled materials are also an important part of Kristen's work, with fabric coming from remnants of evening gowns, favourite dresses and rag bags. The saffron-coloured material in *Rocky Creek,* for example, came from remains of a dress length napthol-dyed by Kristen for her mother.

Some of my best ideas have developed because I couldn't bear to throw away a wonderful fibre or piece of fabric. Recycling appeals to my budget as well as my imagination!

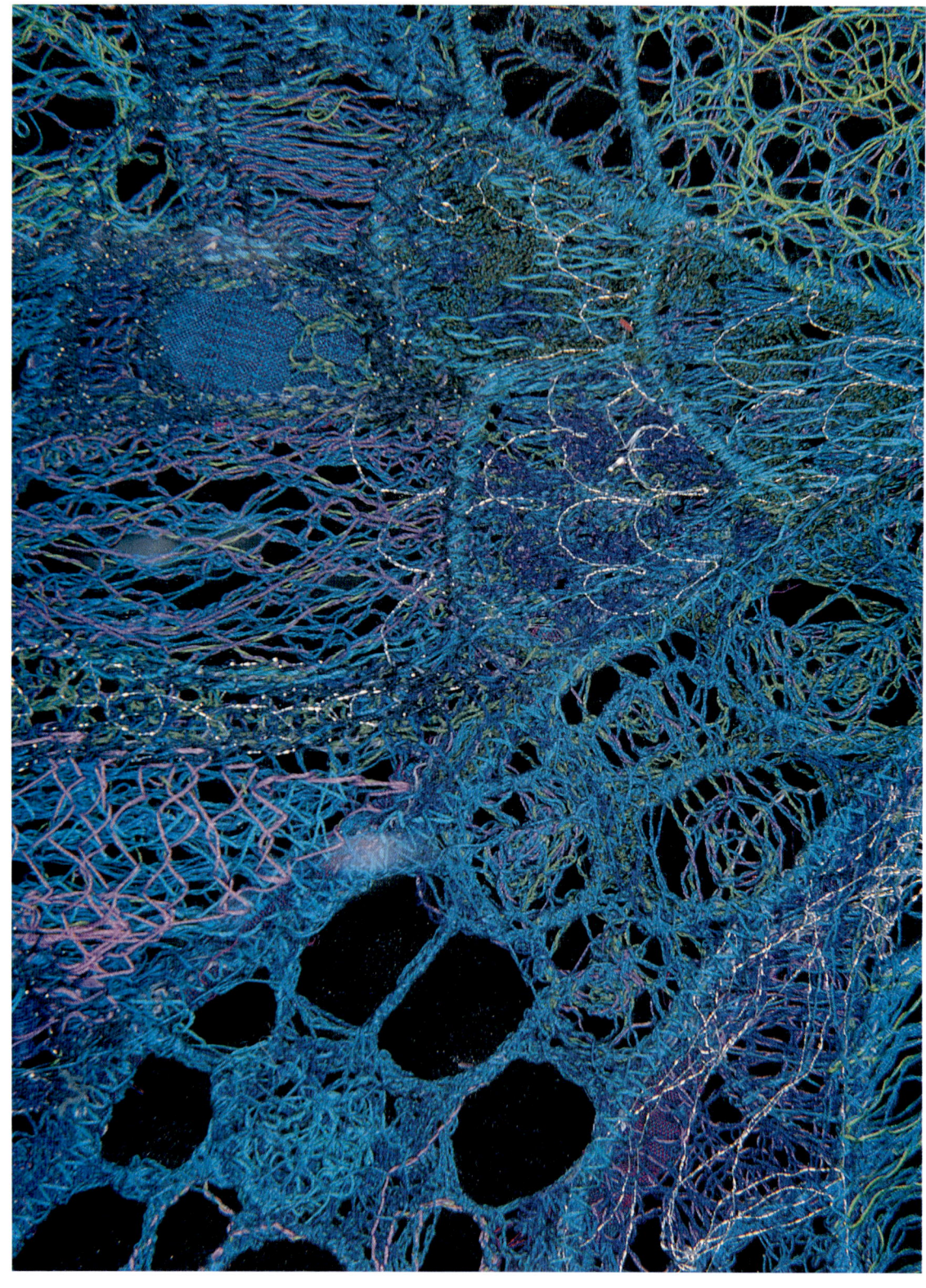

CONTEMPORARY NEEDLEWORK

◄
BUTTERFLY WING *(Detail)*
1989, 250mm x 300mm

machine embroidery, polyester and cotton threads, silk scraps and ravelled threads, metallic embroidery threads
photographer: Eardley Lancaster

▲
FUNGUS
1989, 300mm x 300mm

machine embroidery, silk organza, polyester and cotton threads, mounted on perspex
photographer: Eardley Lancaster

Patrick Snelling

A robust and wilful embellisher of surfaces

Computer technology is used as a creative device in the work of Patrick Snelling. Images are hand drawn and then scanned into the computer for further enhancement and to work out ideas for printing and selecting colours. From the computer printout the image is redrawn and further developed, sometimes using the photocopier for enlargement and for repeating formats:

Nothing is sacred. No labour-saving device is spared to achieve the results I want.

The majority of Patrick's work is screen printed using reactive dyes and pigment inks, with photographic and hand-painting techniques used later to enhance the design. Materials are machine stitched onto calico and wadding to achieve a three dimensional effect. Having no formal training in the use of the sewing machine, Patrick's method is free and unconventional:

I tend to use my machine like a pencil, a robust and wilful embellisher of surfaces, equally decorative and destructive. The actual physical aspect of joining a variety of surfaces and structures together, binding them and enhancing their respective properties, confers upon the work a degree of chance and optimism. Will it work?

VESTIGIAL VENEZIA
1988, 350mm x 400mm x 30mm

screen printed silk, machine stitched with the addition of paper and wire
photographer: Brett Martin

A SENSE OF PLACE

ANGELS (*Detail*)
1988, 300mm x 350mm x 30mm

screen printed silk and cotton, feathers, acetate,
machine stitchery

CONTEMPORARY NEEDLEWORK

▲
ORNAMENTAL SKIRT
1990, 400mm x 350mm x 40mm

screen printed cotton, machine stitched, wire form and object trivia
photographer: John Storey

Overleaf left IDEAL WORLD
1991, 400mm x 35mm x 40mm

screen printed felt, silk and cotton, machine stitching

Overleaf right ANGEL WITH A TORN HEART
1988, 350mm x 300mm x 30mm

screen printed cotton, tissue paper, machine stitched

CONTEMPORARY NEEDLEWORK

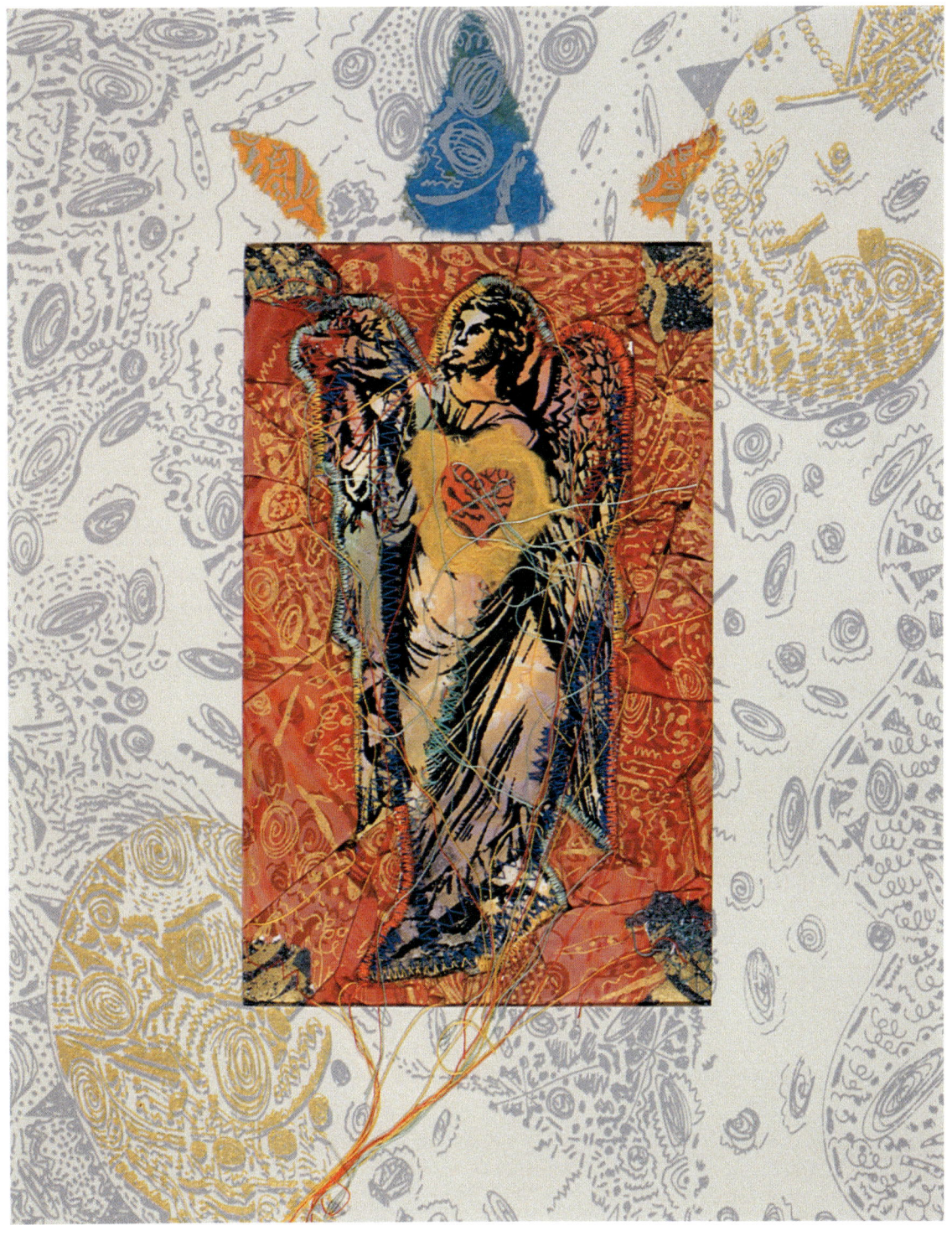

ANGELA ROSSEN

Style, tradition and method: a meeting

The idea of combining painting with textile work first came to Angela Rossen on a painting trip to Greece. Captivated by the lavish decoration of the Orthodox Church vestments and the more humble traditional village needlework, she created a series of paintings that were embellished with embroidery and beading — a meeting of styles, traditions and methods.

The image is built up in stages beginning with the drawing using charcoal, coloured pencil, watercolour or all three:

Drawing and painting are one process in my mind, so I work directly onto the fabric without tracings.

This way the loose lines of the drawing are part of the finished work.

Acrylic paint with transparent washes and thick impasto are then painted on, and onto this surface a variety of coloured threads — cotton, silk, viscose and metallic — are stitched. In the final stage, individual beads are sewn on.

Angela brings all these different media together by using close tonal and colour relationships, preferring to work in monochrome or near monochrome:

Sometimes it may be difficult to see from a distance if a particular colour mark was made with pencil, paint or thread. I enjoy that ambiguity.

JO'S JOHN DOREY
1989, 680mm x 550mm

acrylic and watercolour paint with cotton metallic and viscose threads on cotton, applied beading, from the Ghirardi collection
photographer: Dirk Wittenberg

Helen Baldwin

Vastness and detail: the land and petit point

Helen began her creative life as a watercolour painter, but was inspired to take up needlework when she visited the home of Australian painter Norman Lindsay in Springwood in the Blue Mountains west of Sydney. Watching Rose Lindsay embroidering a screen, Helen was inspired to take up the art form herself and has been addicted to it ever since.

The people and landscape of Central Australia have a special fascination for Helen — people, cultures, her own observations, and a unique light to be captured in fibre:

The Central Australian earth is fine and powdery and soon churned up by cattle. The dust hangs in the air and everything is viewed through a haze of pink. I tried to capture in petit point the dignity of the old people and the shyness and delight of the children.

Helen works in very fine stitching — approximately eleven stitches to one centimetre. Her painterly legacy is clear, and so she sorts the colours of the embroidery cotton in natural daylight as colour accuracy is very important, mixing colours as they are mixed on a palette. However, she prefers to do the embroidering at night by the light of a draughter's lamp.

MAN OF AUSTRALIA
c1973, 740mm x 520mm

petit point

A SENSE OF PLACE

SUNDAY AT PEARL BEACH
1985, 700mm x 510mm

appliqué and free machine embroidery
photographer: Syd Langford

Pat Langford

Our allotted spaces

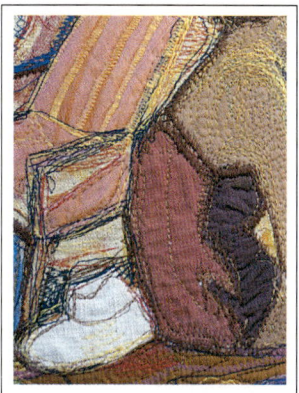

Pat Langford likes to explore light, depth, relationships and spaces of familiarity with her threads and fabrics. The levels of seeing from one place into another, from doorway to room, from shore to sea, and into and behind waterfalls, are played out upon her pieces.

In Pat's canvas work *Still Life at Isabel's*, she records the interior of a friend's house, looks at *the enclosed space we are allotted on this planet*, and allows different sized canvas to represent layers of friendship. Cotton and velvet yarn allow the richness of the life-symbolic bowl of fruit to come through. The beach is another important theme, where people and building up layers of tone and movement create life and interest, as in *Sunday at Pearl Beach*. Finally, light permeates all of this work, and in *Pink Light at Waterfall* the glow of sunset and the fracturing of the light in the Northern Territory's Kakadu rainforest is suggested by endless circles of stitch that break up the surface — light and needle converge.

STILL LIFE AT ISABEL'S
1984, 430mm x 360mm

canvas work using wool, knitting cotton and
velvet yarn
photographer: Syd Langford

CONTEMPORARY NEEDLEWORK

PINK LIGHT AT WATERFALL
1991, 660mm x 560mm

layered fabric, embroidery

Rose Halliday-Smith

The fibrous untidiness of nature

Some designs are carefully planned, but most of Rose Halliday-Smith's work just 'grows' from assembled components. The fabric, specific shapes and printed images are pinned onto a board and juggled until the picture starts to emerge: *This part is full of surprises; some I gloat over, others take days to resolve. Pieces tend to creep out of the picture plane — I don't argue! These extensions create a link with the wall on which the work will hang.*

The presentation of her work is very important — mostly it is allowed to hang simply from a single timber support. She believes that by stretching fabric onto a frame and turning edges in, the sensual appeal of textiles is lost: *Layers of fabric and quilting give any necessary bulk and strength, and exposed raw edges have the blended, softening effect of a brush stroke and show the true nature of woven cloth.*

Having moved to a rainforest area of Queensland, the local environment came to dominate Rose's work. Exotic birdlife and her own vigorously growing garden became favourite subjects: *As I battled to control the creeping green giants of my garden, my work became overcrowded with shredded and layered textiles that so easily echo the fibrous untidiness of nature in this tropical area.*

MUSK LORIKEETS *(Detail)*
1990, 990mm x 1397mm
cotton and polyester fibre and polyester threads, polyester fibre with furnishing velvet, machine and hand stitching

A SENSE OF PLACE

THE SEA AND THE MOON
(Antikythera Series)
1986, 700mm x 900mm

embroidery on silk, blueprint, dyes
photographer: Eric Algra

ALVENA HALL

Mystery and regeneration

Much of Alvena Hall's needlework centres on unifying themes, each work exploring a range of issues and images suggested by the central idea.

The South Australian Ash Wednesday bushfires of 1983 were the basis for the *Regeneration Series.* Choosing to focus on a small nature reserve, Alvena recorded in six works the devastation of the fire through to the gradual process of renewal. *Regeneration 1: Fire Storm* depicts the height of the destruction. Hand and machine quilting is used as well as dyes painted over stencils. The leaves are machine embroidered over vanishing muslin, and wired.

Her next series, *The Antikythera Instrument,* was inspired by the discovery in 1900 of a kind of astronomical calendar found in a shipwreck off the Greek island of Antikythera. A corroded and fragmented wooden box of gears, it was set for 80 B.C., the year it was lost.

The work explores the human need for order, regulation and measurement and draws on images from the Classical past as well as Alvena's own memories of travels in the Aegean.

The project presented a number of technical problems, as Alvena wanted to fix cynatopes (blue-prints) to silk, and needed to find dyes compatible with the blue-printing chemicals. She eventually turned to acid silk dyes from Japan and France, brushed and steamset in the traditional way.

A SENSE OF PLACE

◄ **LAND/SEA/ISLAND** *(Antikythera Series)*
1986, 1200mm x 700mm

embroidery on silk, blueprint, dyes and fabric assemblage
photographer: Eric Algra

► **REGENERATION 1: FIRE STORM** *(Regeneration Series)*
1984, 1200mm x 700mm

dyes, embroidery, quilting

Catherine O'Leary

Patterns in nature

Tropical Fish is a response to the exquisite patterns and colours of the fish of the tropical waters off Queensland. Catherine O'Leary is fascinated by the abstract designs and patterning found throughout the natural world, for example, the patterns and colours of fish, butterflies, flowers and birds.

Catherine first studied the fish in detail and then formed a design in her imagination. No preliminary drawing was done: she embroidered directly onto the canvas.

Inspired by the dedication and perfectionism of craftpeople of earlier centuries, Catherine enjoys the craft traditions of embroidery: *I don't want my work to look like 'Fine Art' paintings. Embroidery is traditionally decorative and I want to use historical techniques, but with my own contemporary designs.*

TROPICAL FISH *(Detail)*
1989, 670mm x 645mm
cross-stitched, stranded cotton and beads

CELEBRATION
1988, 900mm x 1950mm

cotton, procion dyeing, reverse appliqué, hand and machine stitching

Michaela Psaila-Savona

Carnivals of culture

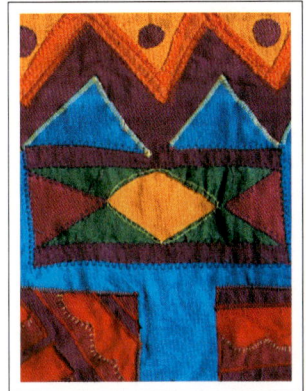

A fascination with Middle America, Indo-America and Euro-America informs much of the work of Michaela Psaila-Savona. She is intrigued by religious and other celebrations, and their expression in textiles: the Mayan symbolic use of colour, for example, where black symbolised war, blue represented sacrifice and yellow signified food. In her own work colour is chosen both for symbolic and for purely aesthetic reasons.

She investigates colouring methods for her fabric through the procion dyeing method, which requires complex processing with dye, soda ash and salt solutions, and she further uses many embroidery techniques of the Aztecs and Incas, such as Mola — reverse appliqué.

A South American Cuna Indian superstition that perfect stitching is unlucky amuses Michaela and has led her to spend hours hand stitching to fully explore this idea. Many levels of spirituality and culture, from imagery to the potential for humour are explored — colour and detail express the interrelations of cultures.

The South American love of carnivals and festivals is a favourite subject for her art work, one that fits her own notions of life and vitality:

Celebration is very important to me, as life and art should be celebrated. Each piece of my work relives many thoughts, superstitions and most of all reflects a love of these lost cultures.

◀

ORANGE PRAYER MAT III
1988, 460mm x 900mm

cotton, procion dyeing, reverse appliqué, hand and machine stitching

▼

PRAYERMAT REGAL I
1988, 540mm x 1130mm

velvet, taffeta and satin, reverse appliqué, machine embroidery, hand and machine stitching

▲
REJOICE *(Detail)*
1988, 1.2m x 2.5m

cotton, procion dyeing, reverse appliqué, hand and machine stitching

A SENSE OF PLACE

GEORGE'S CENTENARY MURAL
1980, 2.4m x 1.5m

mixed media

photographer: Micheal du Jardin

Hester Hopkins

Co-operative creativity

A major project for Hester Hopkins was the designing and co-ordinating of the *George's Centenary Mural* in 1979. This embroidery was a gift to Georges of Melbourne from the Embroiderers' Guild of Victoria, to commemorate the store's centenary.

It was also an opportunity to raise the public profile and status of needlework, and demonstrate that the medium could be as effective aesthetically as more traditional art forms, if designed to be viewed from a distance as well as at close quarters.

George's facade is depicted in three dimensions in the centre of the mural with figures representing 100 years of fashion flowing in and out of the store.

Different sections and features of the total design were embroidered by eighty volunteers throughout Victoria. Each volunteer was given a photocopy of their selected section or item, background fabric, flesh-coloured for the figures, and advice on select techniques to use to blend with the total design. The entire background was embroidered in appliqué on a large embroidery frame. Trees were created by adding french knots — using a mixture of fibres, colours and textures — to fly wire.

When completed, the sections were brought to the studio to be applied. Features on the face were then suggested by isolated stitches or left blank, taking on the appearance and personality of relatives or friends. One particularly buxom figure from the turn of the century came to bear a remarkable resemblance to a former headmistress of Hester's. A full year in production, the mural is a celebration of co-operative creativity.

CONTEMPORARY NEEDLEWORK

▲ GEORGE'S CENTENARY MURAL
(Detail)

▶ GEORGE'S CENTENARY MURAL
(Detail)

◀ GEORGE'S CENTENARY MURAL
(Detail)

A SENSE OF PLACE

GABRIELLA VERSTRAETEN

Movement and abstraction

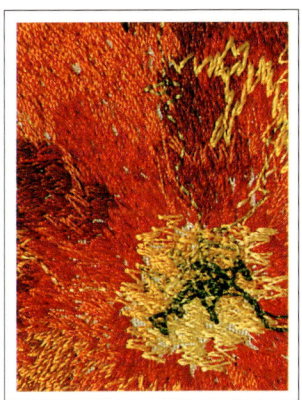

Gabriella Verstraeten's reason for taking up needlework is simple: *The love of embroidery. I create my designs to explore the medium. My work reflects my love of fabric and patterns — it is about creating a visually rich and exciting surface. The fabrics are so appealing, so exciting. I try to produce pieces which are a joyous celebration of this.*

Whilst many artists try to achieve realism in their artwork, Gabriella wants to attract people because of the abstract qualities of her work: *I want them to appreciate the combination of fabrics and unusual colours. I want them to be absorbed by the rhythms of the repetitive motifs, the movements the patterns create.*

Most of Gabriella's work is machine embroidered combined with fabric manipulation, that is, appliqué, layering, cutback, padding and sculpting. Although Gabriella has an 'art for art's sake' approach to her work, she nevertheless enjoys creating work that is practical and useful, such as embellishments on garments, hats, bags, shoes and jewellery. She even embroiders her correspondence.

I love it when people want to reach out and touch the embroidery. To be fascinated by the surface. These kind of feelings and attractions do not occur when we look at paintings or drawings. With embroidery there is more and I want to exploit it.

POPPIES *(Detail)*
1991, 240mm x 350mm
machine embroidered panel on silk shantung base
photographer: Gene Verstraeten

LITANY TO BAST *(Detail)*
1991, 550mm x 750mm

*mixed media, straight stitch and running stitch.
Bast was the Egyptian goddess of mental
healing, intuition and generosity, depicted with
the head of a cat. Her sacred colour was
turquoise, which dominates the colour scheme*

Heather Johns

Magic, ritual, ceremony

Myth, Magic and Ritual is the theme of Heather Johns' latest series of work. She explores human beliefs and rituals from Palaeolithic death cults, through the flowering of the cultures of Babylon and Egypt and up to present day rituals of Africa: *I try to invoke a sense of time and place; to allow the viewer to glimpse, and hopefully respond to, the ceremony, the wonder and the drama surrounding a particular myth or ritual.*

The works evolve by two main processes: the research and associated visual images, and the manipulation of fabrics, threads, colour and structure as the background is created.

Myth, Magic and Ritual is presented as a sequence of individual tabloids, each depicting one aspect of the narrative. Heavyweight, coloured pastel paper is used as the base as it is strong but still allows easy stitching. The backgrounds are usually silk or occasionally handmade plant paper or cotton and are stitched down using hand dyed silk threads and metallics. The silk fabric is often dyed, rotted and always frayed to allow a visual blending with surrounding elements. Gold leaf is used in most of the works to add richness, light and a sense of preciousness to symbolise the precious wisdom of each culture.

Heather describes stitchery as 'vital': *It is not the dominant element of my work but it is what binds the whole image together, literally as well as visually. The stitches are very simple; I rely on the viewer's knowledge that a stitch binds things together to make a whole; there is no need for complexity.*

CONTEMPORARY NEEDLEWORK

◀ OFFERINGS FOR THE JOURNEY
(Detail) 1991, 550mm x 750mm

mixed media, straight stitch and cross stitch. Depicting the ritual burial of the leader of a Palaeolithic tribe, this work is stencilled using ochre, sienna and red oxide powders and liberally 'smoked' to create an atmosphere reminiscent of a cave

▲ THE DESCENT OF ISHTAR
(Detail) 1991, 550mm x 750mm

mixed media, straight stitch and running stitch. Ishtar, the Babylonian goddess of love and fertility, descends to the underworld to find her lover Tammuz, the god of vegetation. The underworld is represented by a rectangle of black paper with radiating black and gold threads producing a tunnelling effect

ANNEMIEKE MEIN

A statement of respect and love

Annemieke Mein has a strong commitment to the preservation of the Australian environment and sees all her work, whether free-standing sculptures, wall panels or 'wearables', as a statement of respect and love for the environment.

Her main subjects are native flora and fauna and each work is preceded by hours of research, observation and documentation. Countless sketches and cartoons are made before the full-size layout is designed. Only then are paints, fibres, fabrics and threads selected, and the sewing begun. Subjects are depicted larger than life. This not only enhances the visual impact by allowing a varying of relief angles and sculptural levels; it also allows detailed textural variations and subtle colour combinations:

Minute details, such as the inside of a bird's beak, the interplay of light on an insect's wing venation, or the glistening of fish scales underwater, are deliberately accentuated to capture an event or experience and the emotion that the subject has aroused in me.

BASS STRAIT — FISHING:
BIG FISH/SMALL FRY
1982, 400mm x 500mm

paint, silk and stitches on linen

Paul O'Connor

The cultural rubbish dump of the soul

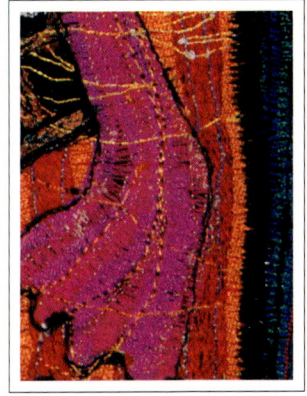

Paul O'Connor sees his stitched, stuffed, encrusted 'drawings' as tactile manifestations of diary images. Pictures of thoughts, feelings, events build up from the 'cultural rubbish dump' of the city and his studio, allowing him to explore themes, colours, techniques and layers of meanings.

Linking his vibrant view of the world to the practical and functional, Paul likes to continue the tradition of all household objects being works of art. The viewer is as important as the creator, and so we are invited to touch, use, open, sit on, and ponder his pieces. In terms of process, he is not constrained by method or inspiration — hand work can complement as well as challenge slick designs of the '90s, machine embroidery can be pushed beyond the realms of decorative art. He is not at all restricted by traditional boundaries, and explores autobiography and sensuality, sexuality and domesticity, lured on by various forces:

The bright strange images of Mexican mythology, the work of Mirka Miora and Hundertwasser, avante garde glossy fashion magazines, signs of the zodiac and olde worlde illustrations…it is the eclectic juxtaposition of these factors and more that invade and persuade my thought processes.

I WISH I COULD CHANGE THE WORLD FOR ME *(Detail)*
1991, book cover, 440 mm x 300mm
rayon thread, silk, linen

▲
BOW WOW WOW
1988
machine embroidery, paint

◀
SIT ON MY FACE AND TELL
ME THAT YOU LOVE ME
(Detail: seat cover from chair)
1991, 400mm x 300mm

▶
HAVING TO LISTEN TO MY
LOVE LOVE-MAKING *(Detail)*
1991, book cover, 440mm (open) x 300mm

I WISH I COULD CHANGE THE
WORLD FOR ME *(Detail)*

CONTEMPORARY NEEDLEWORK

ME, ONE IN THE SAME
1991, 360mm x 260mm

papier mâché, rayon thread, found objects, machine stitched

JUDITH PINNELL

Imperial treasures

A recent visit to India has transformed the needlework of Judith Pinnell. Previously, Judith's work was representational, using the soft colours of the English countryside where her interest in textiles first developed. Since her return from India she has developed an interest in simple ethnic designs using the bright satins and silks and the gold threads seen in *Imperial Treasure*.

The *thang-kas* (devotional wall hangings) seen in monasteries in Sikkim left a lasting impression:

There are many Tibetan refugees in Sikkim who have brought their culture and religion with them. Despite being driven from their homeland, they still manage to produce textiles and art that are full of life and vitality.

The background silk of *Imperial Treasure* was hand dyed five times before the right colour was achieved and silk pieces heat fixed onto it. Machine and hand embroidery in gold metallic threads, beads, sequins, gold paint and gold kid used to simulate *Shisha* or mirror work, add to the rich, vivid effect. *I suppose my hanging is really an attempt to recreate the excitement I felt on my travels, from the splendour of the Moghul palaces to the happiness of the Tibetan people who always seemed to be smiling.*

IMPERIAL TREASURE *(Detail)*
1991, 740mm x 540mm

free machine and hand embroidery, block printing, appliqué, hand dyed silk

A SENSE OF PLACE

DOROTHY ROTH

Searching for the essence

Most of Dorothy Roth's work, including *Central Australia*, is inspired by photographs although she sometimes works from memory:
I study the subject for some time in search of the 'essence', and then work on my adaptation of it.

A fascination for inland Australia drew Dorothy to explore the landscape in needlework:
Since childhood I have been drawn to this unspoilt landscape in some mystic sense — the mystery of an ancient land. Creative embroidery has provided a means of expressing this.

Dorothy prefers to work in wool — woollen textiles, fine embroidery wools and homespun, rough slubby yarns — with some cotton threads used for contrast and highlights.

Where possible just one form of stitching is used, as Dorothy finds a variety of stitches distracting. Cretan stitch is a favourite because of its versatility. *Central Australia* is done almost entirely in this stitch, with buttonholing outlining the distant hills. Homespun wool provides the contrast in the foreground.

CENTRAL AUSTRALIA
1988, 200mm x 270mm

stranded cotton on flannel in cretan stitch
photographer: Gene Sparks

A SENSE OF PLACE

SCORCHED TREES
1988, 200mm x 325mm

free machine embroidery on painted fabric

Doreen Curran

Distance, depth and dimension

As a stage setting is how Doreen Curran thinks of her needlework: *I start at the horizon, then come forward in layers using hand painting, appliqué, quilting and stump work techniques to create distance, depth and dimensions.*

Scorched Trees is a response to the ravages of a bush fire through a forest of gums near Mount York in the Blue Mountains, west of Sydney: *I was impressed not only with the brilliant colours and the silent stillness, but also with the beginnings of regrowth and regeneration.*

The background was first hand painted and then prepared with a number of free machine embroidery techniques, while the trees in the foreground were built up with free machine embroidery over threads of linen.

In her other pieces, Doreen has also used various techniques and materials to investigate nature — from organza and silk to calico and linen. By exploring different landscapes and objects, she allows the delicacy and vulnerability of her subject to inform her choices of materials and techniques.

CELIA PLAYER

Creation through destruction

Celia Player takes a radical approach to her embroidery, cutting, tearing, burning, fraying and even melting her fabric to create the desired effect. Her designs are first planned on paper, using drawing and collage. The process is then repeated with fabric that is textured and coloured according to the design scheme — all of the fabric she uses is hand printed and painted — although the design continues to develop intuitively.

Arriving in Australia recently from England, Celia has a special responsiveness to the particular features of the Australian environment. The ceremonial body markings of some Aboriginal tribes, modern Sydney architecture, the intense light, have all influenced her work.

The triptych *So ... this is Australia* undertaken soon after her arrival, depicts the initial insecurities of migration, the transition to exploration of her new country, and a final reaching out for the soul of Australia without letting go of the homeland.

SO...THIS IS AUSTRALIA
(triptych)
1990, 600mm x 340mm

hand painted and printed silk and silk chiffon, collage, machine embroidery

Overleaf left SEEK OUT HER DEPTHS *(triptych, Detail)*

Overleaf right AND MAKE HER SPIRIT KNOWN *(triptych, Detail)*

A SENSE OF PLACE

RAINFOREST
1983, 1030mm x 640mm

*three level needle weaving on hand woven wool
with quilting and stitchery*

CYNTHIA SPARKS

Depths of design: weaving the rainforest

A biologist by training, Cynthia Sparks has both a deep understanding and an empathy with plants, bush landscapes and the colours of nature. Having worked with thread for a long time, she has also explored possibilities for communicating this fascination, for showing textures and contrasts and layers of landscapes. Cynthia prefers to express this landscape, however, by looking at the particular, the detailed, the small — the leaf rather then the whole tree, the form of a piece of bark — to represent a whole place. The materials themselves, and other media such as photography, add further to this complexity, suggesting themes and approaches themselves.

Accordingly, her piece *Rainforest* grows both from the blue/green of transparencies taken deep within the rainforest, the unevenness of handspun and dyed wools, and collections of silks. To incorporate all these elements, Cynthia has developed interesting and adaptable techniques. Three levels are formed from one piece of tabby weave; alternate threads are cut on either warp or weft and stripped back to expose threads that can then be woven, wrapped or buttonholed into new patterns. Finally, the finished piece is mounted in a box frame to allow light, shadow and depth to be part of the rainforest. This layered needleweaving is intriguing as it allows layers of meaning and interpretation to grow from basic materials.

A SENSE OF PLACE

HOMETOWN
1991, 550mm x 800mm

hand embroidery, silk, clay tiles

Mirjam Koenig

Silk magic

Emigrating from Switzerland to Australia ten years ago, Mirjam Koenig's recollection of her homeland remains a feature of her work. *Hometown* reflects her love of the European medieval town: *where roads are narrow and the houses stand tall and close, often surrounded by a wall, a defence against intruders and a sign of unity. I love the warm, homely face of such a settlement, the cosiness about it. And I am fascinated by the mystery which is part of any old place where generations have lived over many centuries.*

Nazca Lines, by contrast, is based on the group of huge animal figures and geometric forms scratched into the desert north of Nazca in southern Peru. The figures are virtually indecipherable at ground level but are plainly visible from the air.

For me, the Nazca Lines are a fascinating statement of a long gone people, a form of communication: but with whom? The mystery remains.

The method of dyeing and embroidery used for both pieces is quite unusual. Mirjam first hand sews the various pieces of silk onto the undyed backing, each piece subsequently taking up to three weeks to embroider. She then paints the dyes onto the needlework, all too well aware that after weeks of painstaking work, the whole piece could be ruined in a matter of minutes:

If it works though, the excitement of seeing the embroidery and the textures of the silk pieces come alive is magic.

Finally, once steamset the pieces are further embroidered and objects such as beads, clay or moulded paper elements are added. Individual areas are painted again or enhanced with gilt polish. The stitches used in the two pieces reproduced here are: straight stitch, french knots, chain stitch, stem stitch, couching, star stitch and cross stitch, while *Nazca Lines* also contains some free machine embroidery.

HOMETOWN *(Detail)*

HOMETOWN *(Detail)*

NAZCA LINES
1991, 550mm x 800mm
*hand and machine embroidery,
silk and clay tiles*

A SENSE OF PLACE

WENDY WRIGHT

Fleeting memories

Not a Bed of Roses I was prompted by a challenge from a textile group Wendy Wright belongs to: create an artwork using three different fabrics, thread, safety pins, beads, feathers, string, wood, paper and stones.

The work grew to become a reflection on twenty years of marriage. Red and yellow roses define happiness and children with fabric weaving representing intertwined lives. Torn netting and areas held together with safety pins symbolises a gradual disintegration.

Much of the inspiration for Wendy's work comes as she hand dyes fabric for use in her needlework: *The colours I create inspire images which more than likely are subliminal; a fleeting memory of something viewed briefly months before.*

Machine embroidery is used for most of her work: *I enjoy the spontaneity and speed of the machine, creating subtle flowing lines and heavier textural areas simply by changing thread and speed.*

NOT A BED OF ROSES I
1991, 140mm x 110mm

machine embroidery with metallic and cotton threads, crochet threads, fabric manipulation, sculptured roses, eyelets, dyed fabrics

A SENSE OF PLACE

BARRIER REEF CORPORATE
WALL *(Detail)*
1991, each panel 100mm x 100mm

machine stitching on acetate

photographer: Eardley Lancaster

Helen Lancaster

Underwater places

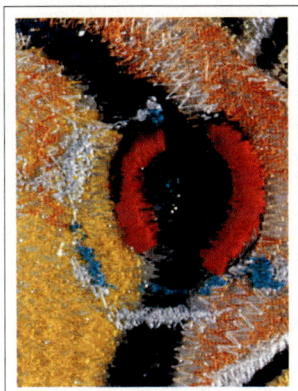

Helen Lancaster's massive project, *The Barrier Reef Corporate Wall*, is still to be completed. At present the wall consists of twenty five tiles, each 100mm x 100mm, but it may grow to three times that size when finished. Using a sewing machine, Helen limited herself to satin, straight or herringbone stitch variations. Each tile is worked on acetate (the material used for shirt boxes), which, because of its transparency and shininess, gives the illusion of water when light catches it. Helen also discovered that the acetate became sculptured by tightening or loosening stitch areas; three dimensional effects could therefore be created, such as hiding fish behind weeds or projecting the arms of an anemone outwards. Helen also tried using two different colours at one time, one in the bobbin and one on the top of the machine, to provide brilliant colour combinations.

This is a memory wall reminding me of the beauty of the Great Barrier Reef, or the magic felt when peering underwater with that first set of goggles. I want people to love and cherish this magical heritage.

A SENSE OF PLACE

BARRIER REEF CORPORATE
WALL *(Detail)*

BARRIER REEF CORPORATE WALL *(Detail)*

A SENSE OF PLACE

MACEDONIAN PROJECT
1991, 1m x 1.2m
hand stitching, wool
photographer: Eardley Lancaster

The Macedonian Project

Piece by piece: images of community

The *Macedonian Project* was designed by Helen Lancaster, but embroidered by a group of Macedonian women calling themselves *Dobrouto*. They invited Helen to design a banner depicting memories of their homeland and their joy in their new country, Australia. The group consisted of Donka Talevska, Cveta Grbevska, Zoja Ribar, Spaca Gorevska, Mara Temelkovska, Luba Markovska, Slavka Bogdanovska and Slavka Kiprovska.

The banner was divided into twelve scenes each 215mm x 255mm with the completed banner 1m x 1.2m.

The women described to Helen memories of their homeland, from pictures of farm life to their love of dancing to pipe music. From these descriptions, Helen painted the designs in gouache and then traced and painted them on the tapestry cloth. Pieced together, the series give a montage view of a community's memories of the past. Contintental stitch with wool was used for the tapestry.

JOAN CHAPPLE

Gentleness and strength

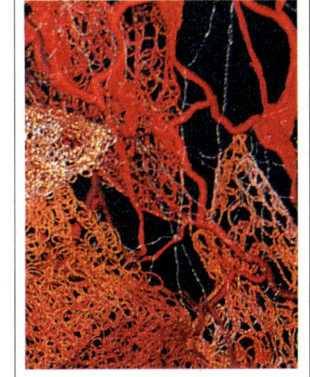

Joan Chapple's work *Shawl* acquired its name because of its shape and size. People began to inquire about the 'shawl' and so the work was christened.

In fact, *Shawl* is a response to the landscape of Central and north-western Australia, completed while Joan was on the other side of the globe, studying in London:

I have a deep feeling for the special places I have visited in Australia; the great strength and power of Uluru (Ayer's Rock) and Katajuta, and the contrasting softness and gentleness of the inland colours at dawn and dusk.

Joan captures this contrast of softness and strength by varying her machining technique throughout the work. Some areas are open and lacey, giving a feeling of gentleness, while others are extremely heavily worked until a very firm self-supporting fabric is achieved. All sections of the piece were machine embroidered onto support fabric held firmly in an embroidery ring until the required texture was gained. The fabric was then washed away leaving the interlocking and overlapping machine threads constituting the fabric of the completed work. Metallic thread gives the feeling of the shimmering strength of the outback during the heat of the day.

SHAWL *(Detail)*
1986, 850mm x 960mm

machine embroidery

Pamela Gaunt

The celebration of raw edges

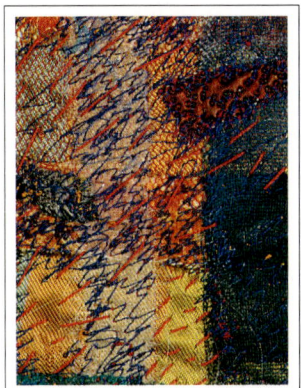

Non-traditional materials are included in much of Pamela Gaunt's needlework creating unusual and dramatic effects. Wood, foil, books, broken needles and the like are combined with old textiles, ornate and heavily embroidered.

Another important concern is to expose the traditional process of textile making into the artwork. Tacking, seams, loose threads and raw edges, traditionally hidden in textile work, are exposed and celebrated:

My concern is to explore the inherent aesthetic qualities of these elements and expose them as part of the work. If a needle breaks during the construction of a work, it is tied into the piece.

Relationships and personal experiences inform much of Pamela's work:

I use the language of materials and stitch to construct layers — to conceal, semi-reveal and expose certain elements.

THREADS OF JOURNEYS *(Detail)*
1991, 970mm x 1250mm
small scale quilt

HEATHER JOYNES

Texture, techniques, landscape

Appliqué, dyed fabric, silk painting and other stitch-work provide background for Heather Joynes's embroidery. Texture, depth and senses of landscape are important to her work, as is nature and from it, inspiration. Heather finds colour, patterns, and form in gardens and in rooftops, in movement of waves and in the texture of ribbons.

The most wonderful thing about embroidery, she finds, is the great diversity of technique. Beginning with hand sewing and functional approaches to the needle, she has come to explore — through her own work, via teaching, and with experience in other media — the visual and tactile effects of hand and machine stitchery, painting and printing. Apart from the therapeutic effects of this form, it has also led her to an interest in antique method, needlework, tools and conservation of the work of artists from other times.

In this piece — *Seascape* — the subtle textures of the place and the sense of movement of bird and wave are conveyed via the dyed wash of blue that is the sky and horizon, the silk ribbons that give depth to the sea and the blue-green stitching that complement them. The bird is a knot of silk ribbon, which links stitches and fabric.

SEASCAPE
1986, 240mm x 200mm

machine embroidery on dyed background

INGA HUNTER

From the forest floor

Moving to the Blue Mountains from inner Sydney proved to be a powerful stimulus for the needlework of Inga Hunter. The forest floor intrigues her:

I am fascinated by the rich layering of what falls to the ground and what accumulates on the various surfaces.

She produced a large number of works based on this theme, of which *Crewel Embroidery* and *Lichen* are two examples. *Stitch to Stitch* has less specific sources of inspiration and stems from Inga's exploration of a variety of techniques and media including etching, woodblock printmaking and drawing.

Inga paints all her embroidery, both before and after stitching, although the first attempts were nerve-racking:

It was difficult to do, in that I was very nervous about putting paint onto something that took hours to stitch — it would be so easy to ruin it. I now paint all my embroidery; in fact I am incapable of working any other way. It is the uneven, interesting painterly quality I like. Commercial embroidery threads are all dyed so evenly and mechanically.

STITCH TO STITCH
1991, 500mm x 700mm

stitchery (satin, seed, straight, fly, french knots), paint, pencil. This work consists of three small layered embroideries mounted on a drawing based on the stitches used in the work.

CONTEMPORARY NEEDLEWORK

◄ **CREWEL EMBROIDERY**
1982, 350mm x 250mm

painted embroidery (satin stitch) on wool, set into handmade paper

▲ **LICHEN** *(Detail)*
1985, 200mm x 200mm

handmade paper, stitchery (french knots, detached french knots, straight stitch and seeds), paint, wood

A SENSE OF PLACE

CHERUBS *(Detail from smock)*
1991, 580mm x 360mm

printing and hand stitching onto
a silk smock

Sonja Armstrong

The stitching of angels

Art and architecture have been important sources of inspiration for the work of Sonja Armstrong. Greek columns have become column dresses with stone capitals translated into the delicacy of fibre and thread. More recently Sonja has discovered the artists of the Renaissance and painting, sculpture and architectural elements have formed designs on jackets and dresses.

Her recent work, *Cherubs,* was inspired both by Raphael's depiction of babies and cherubs and Sonja's own personal excitement at the recent birth of two nieces.

Usually, Sonja's work is machine stitched for it's richness of colour, density and solidarity. The subject of *Cherubs* — the children, the lightness — called for a more gentle approach. Hand sown running stitch was chosen to create a rich texture that is subtle and powerful at the same time:
What could be more simple, yet strikingly effective than the most basic stitch — the running stitch.

STEPHANIE WOOD

Dreaming interiors

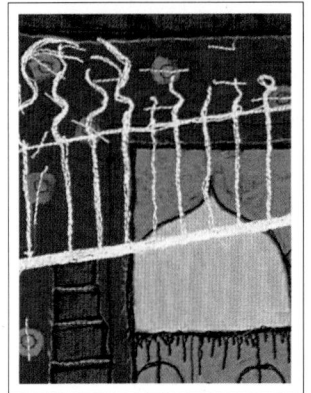

Stephanie Wood draws her images from a variety of places, from dream worlds to reality, from staircases to winning the Pools, and transforms them with fibres and textiles. She is particularly concerned with exploring her past and relationships with people close to her, especially her grandmother. In the series shown here, it is an interior world, of dreams and thoughts, that dominates. Colours and depths of design are used to extend emotions: muted colours evoke a dream state, and vibrant reds show a fantasy world.

Stephanie begins by dyeing all of her silks, and then uses a rough plan and layers of material, cutting, shaping and sewing details until the whole painstaking process is complete. She also enjoys using bead work, bringing her embroidery into relief by the use of 'puffing' techniques, and experimenting with dyeing processes.

The Red Carpet is the first work in a series based on a haunting recurring dream. It shows a room in a house, the first room she enters. The red is brooding, and cut-away techniques serve to emphasise layers of meaning and interpretation. Figures in the carpet are stitched in dramatically. In the 'untitled' piece, with stairs entwined and figures looking on, the next stage in the dream is given substance by using reverse appliqué and machine stitching. The stairs are solid and mysterious, possibly representing, according to Stephanie, the beginning of a journey or a life, whose levels continue on and around.

UNTITLED *(Dream Series)*
1991, 500mm x 335mm x 20mm

silk, canvas, gauze, reverse appliqué, machine embroidery
photographer: Victor France

A SENSE OF PLACE

THE HOUSE WITH THE RED
CARPET *(Dream Series)*
1991, 525mm x 430mm x 20mm

silk, canvas, gauze, reverse appliqué, machine
embroidery
photographer: Victor France